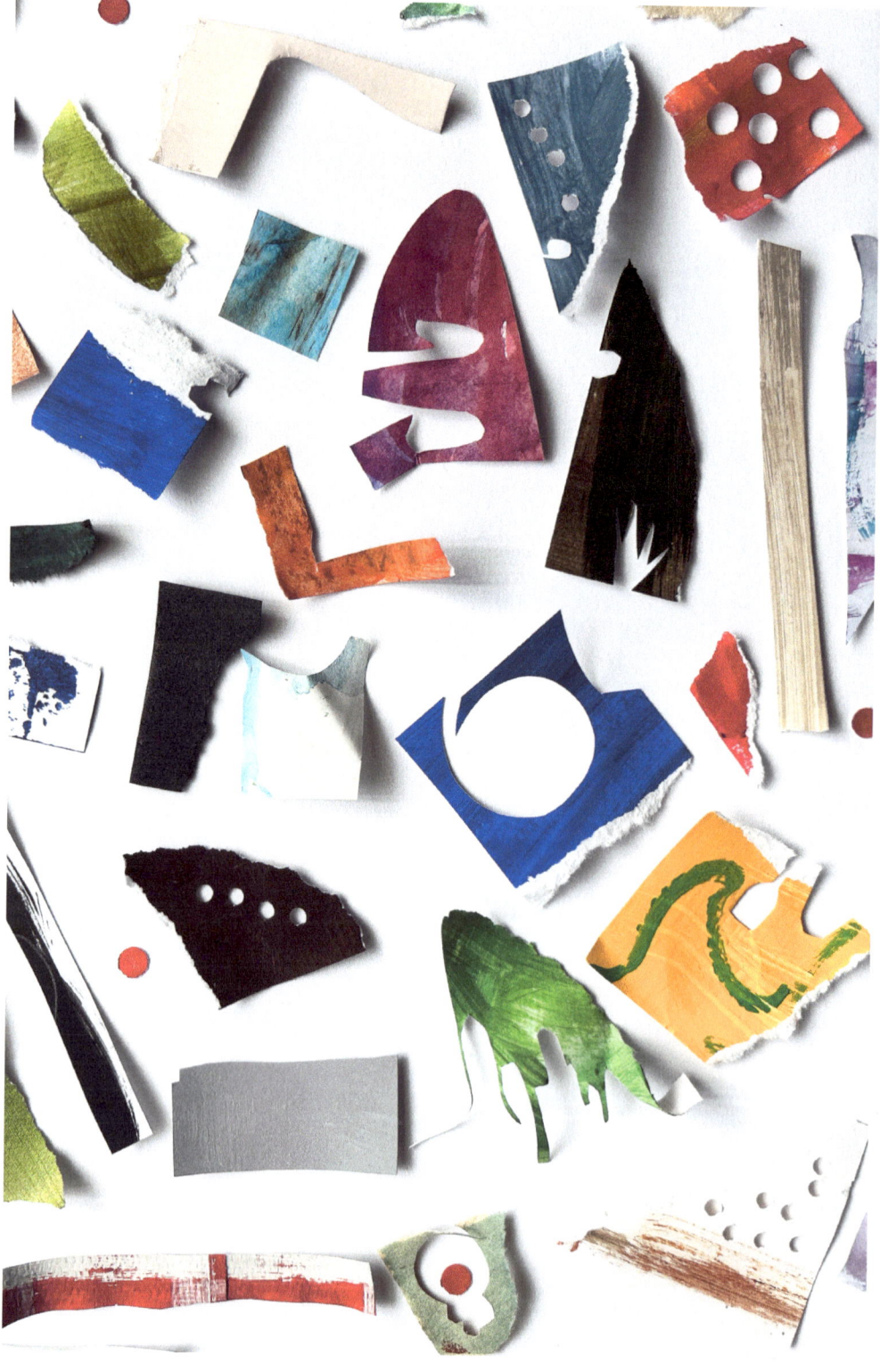

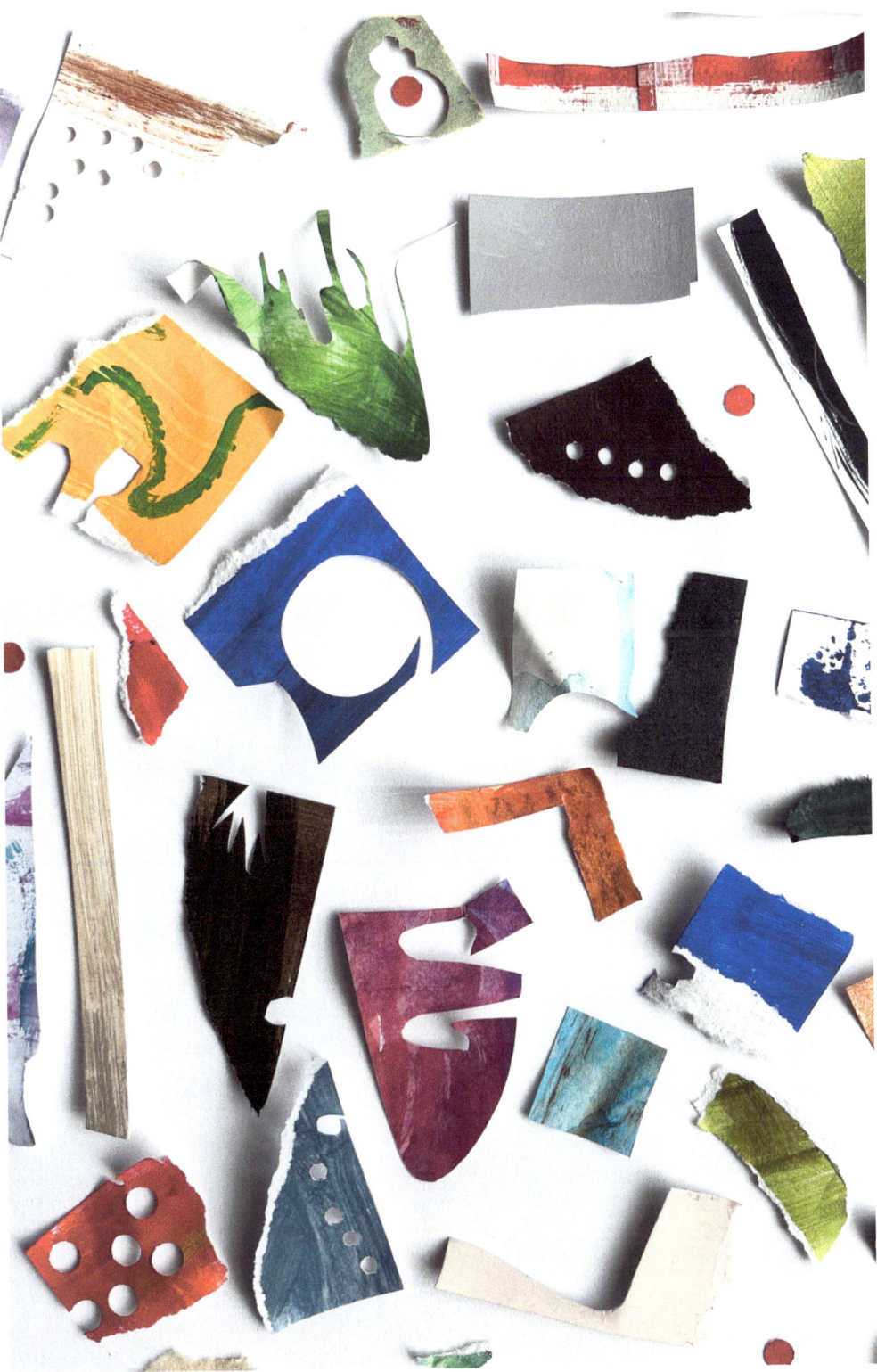

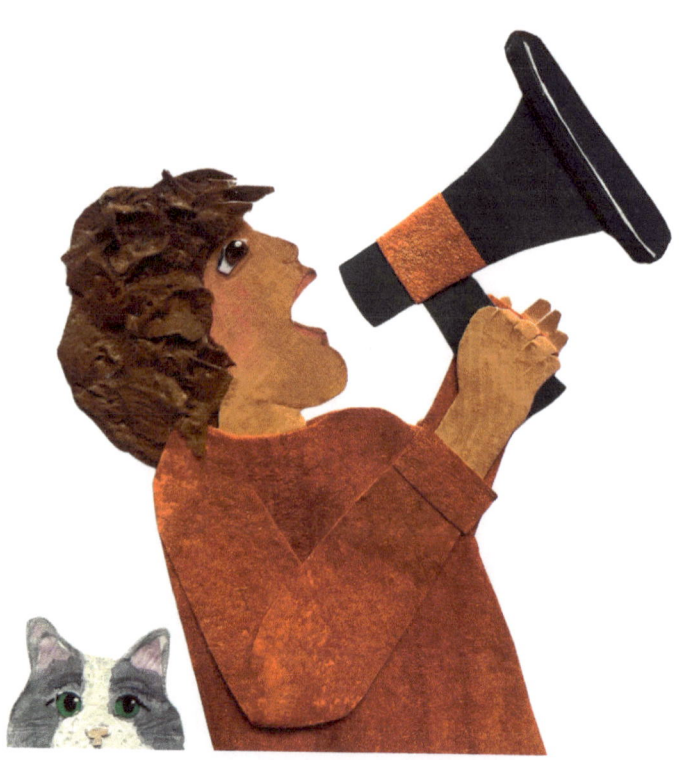

ACTION! ABCs WITH CAT AND FRIENDS

WORDS AND SNIPS BY
LAURA HOMSEY

FOR CLARA, ALEC, AND
BEATRICE
3 KIDS WHO REALLY KNOW
HOW TO MOVE!

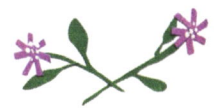

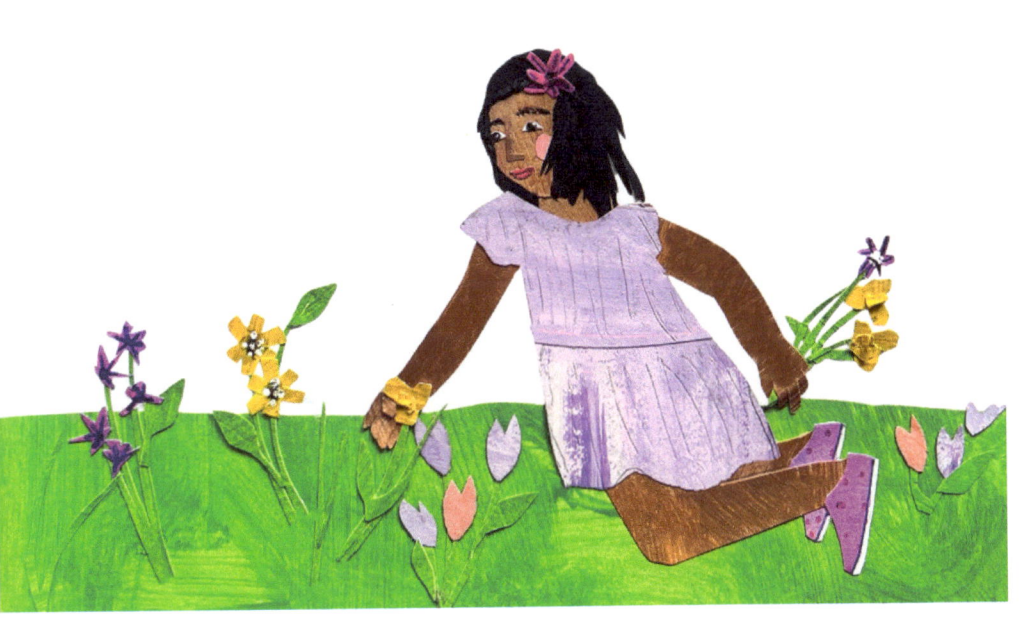

A IS FOR ACT

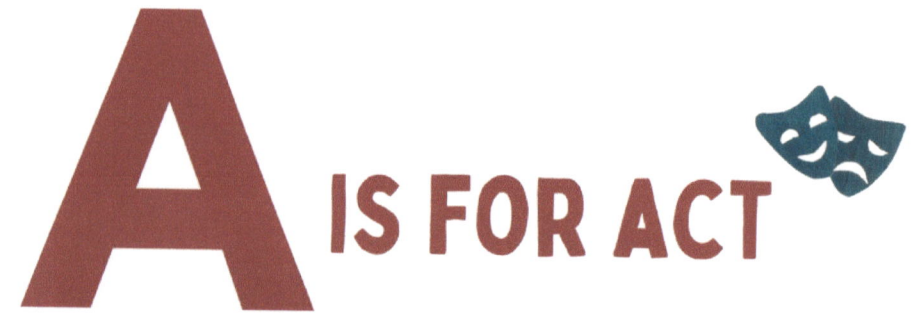

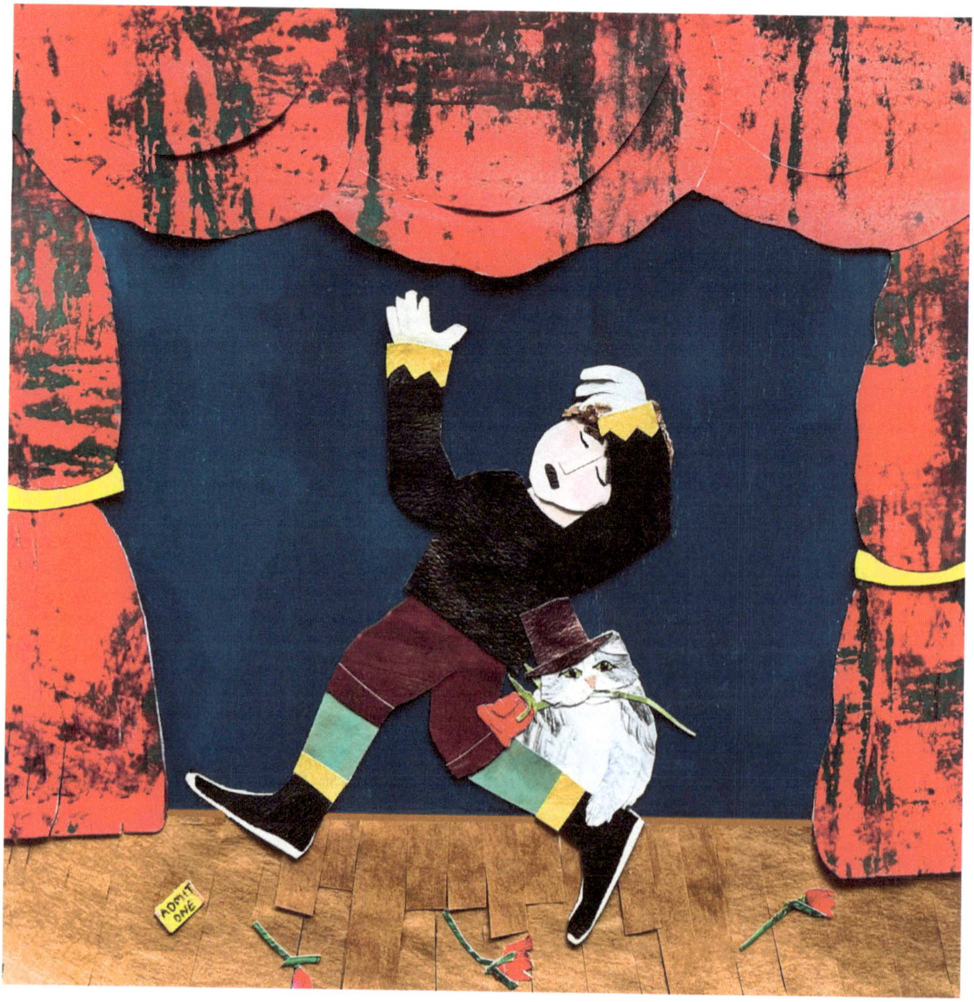

AND THE AUDIENCE CLAPPED!

B IS FOR BUILD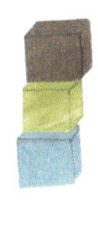

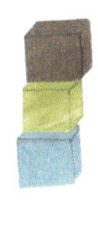

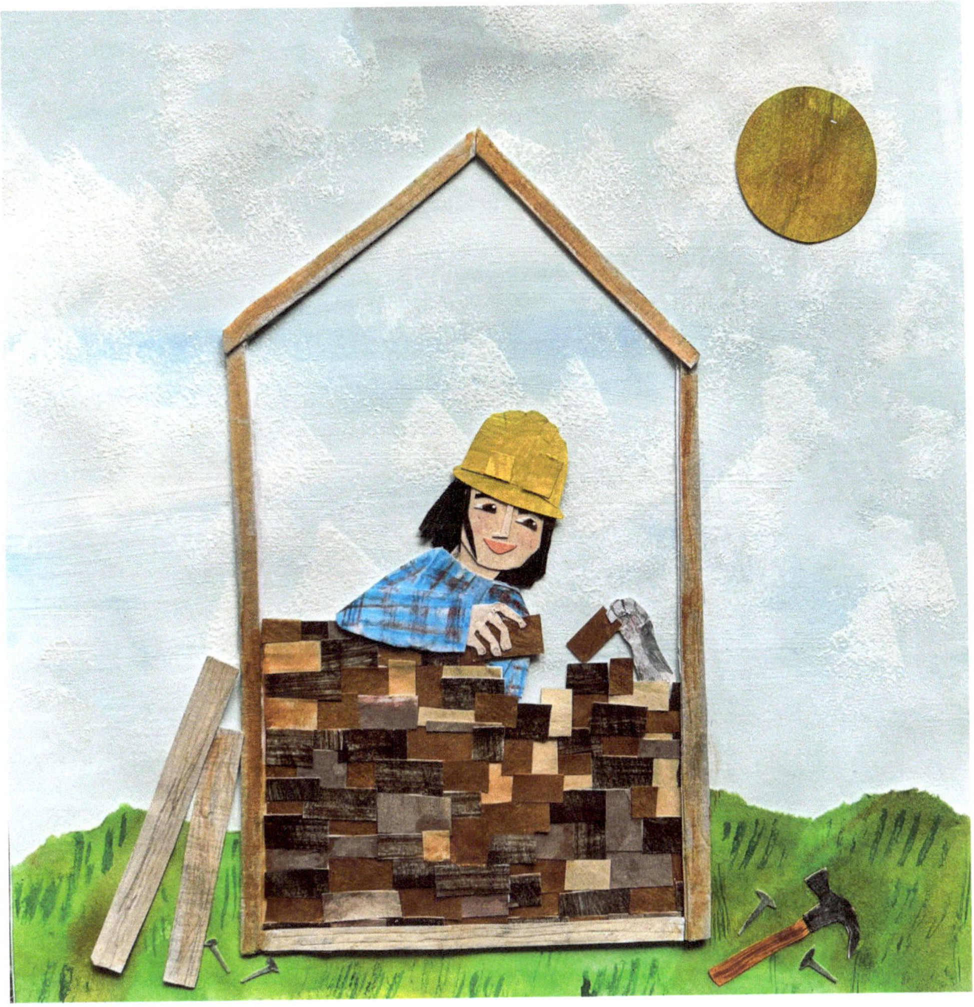

SO THEY HAMMERED AND DRILLED.

C IS FOR COLOR

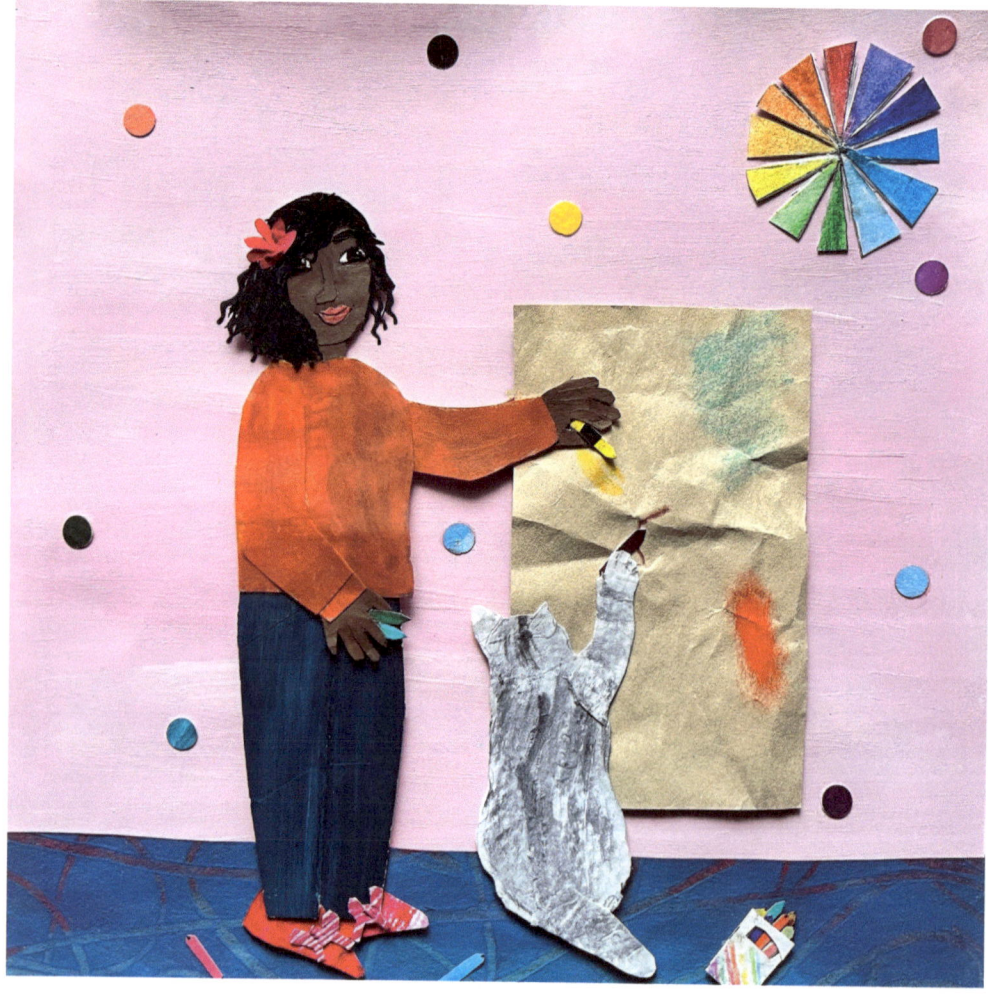

SO MANY MARKERS, HAND ME ANOTHER!

D IS FOR DRINK

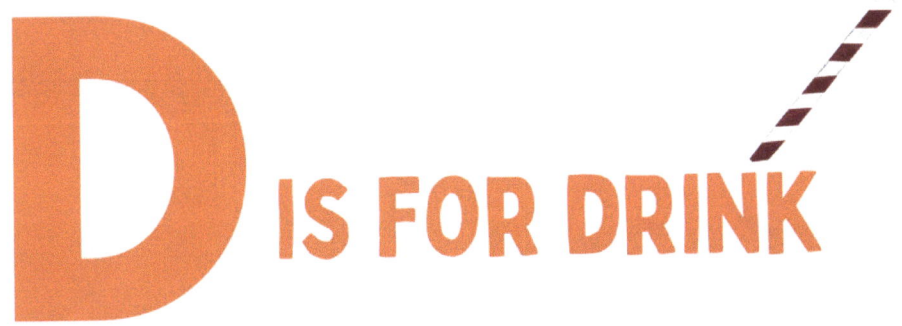

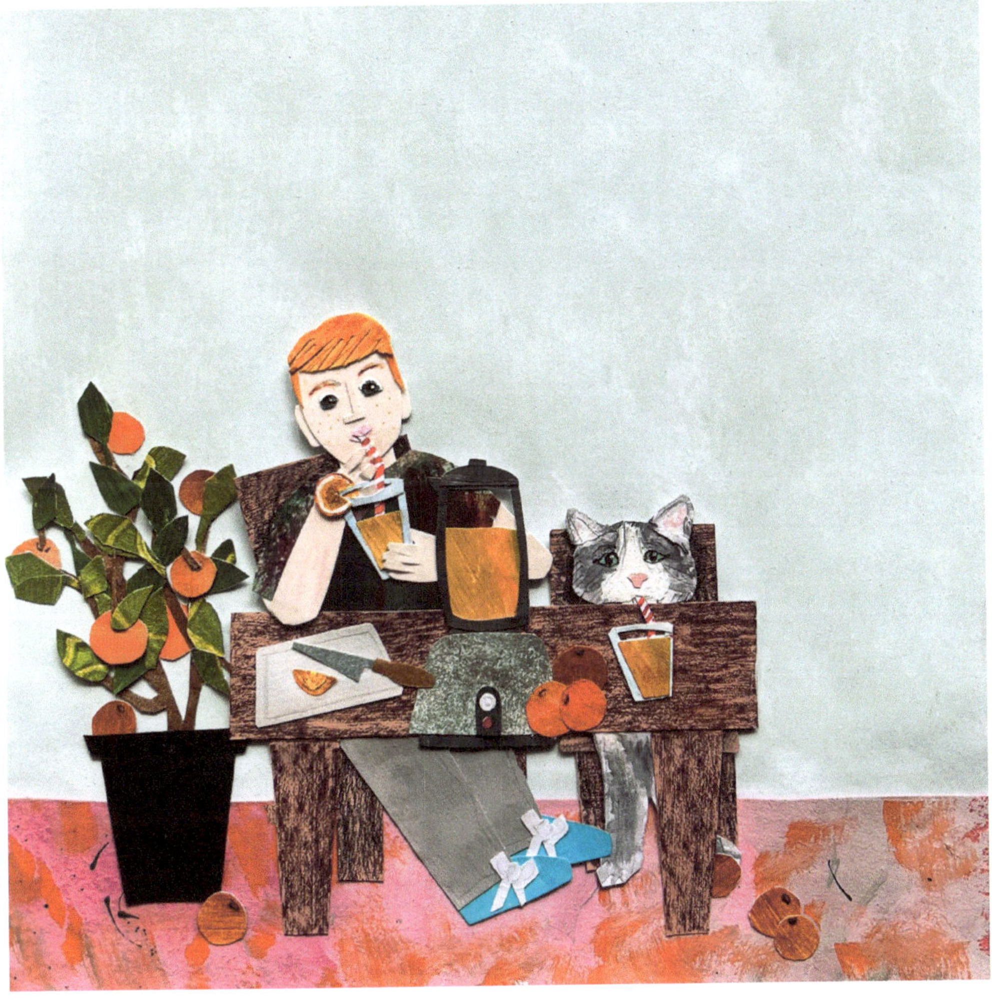

TASTES SO GOOD IT'S WORTH A *CLINK*.

E IS FOR EAT

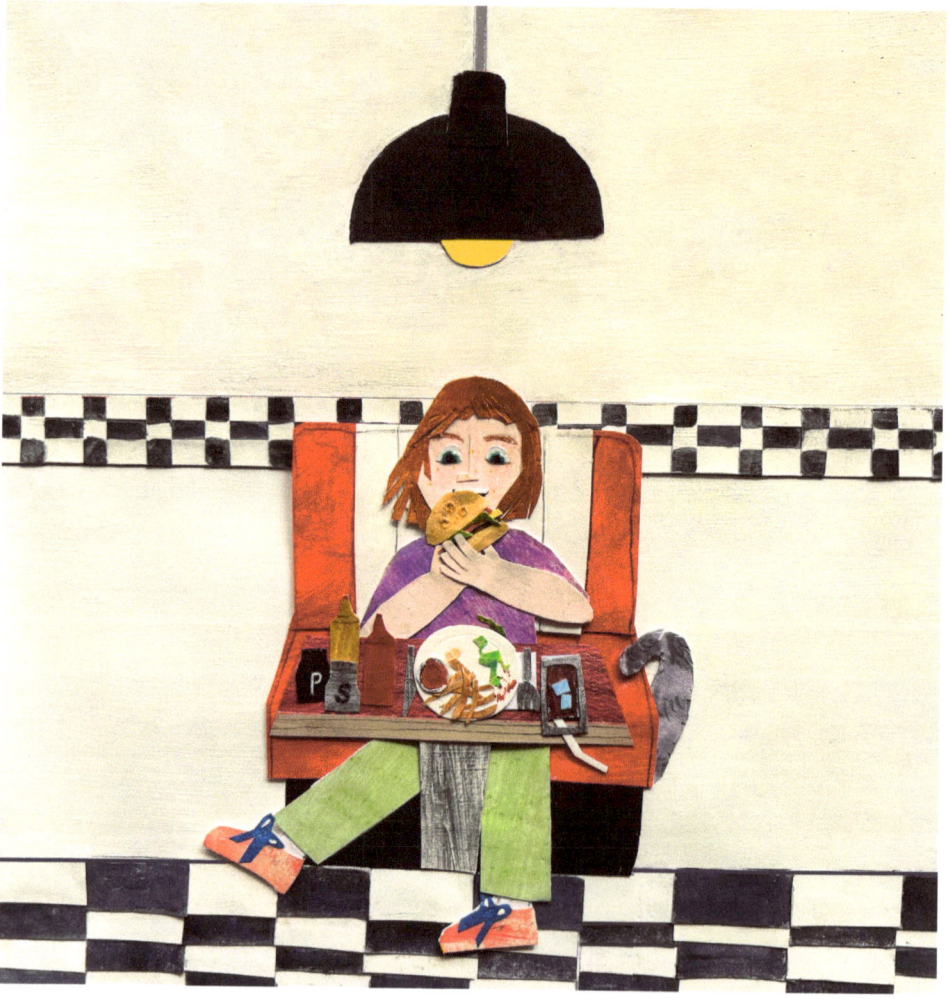

FOOD IS READY, WHAT A TREAT!

F IS FOR FROWN

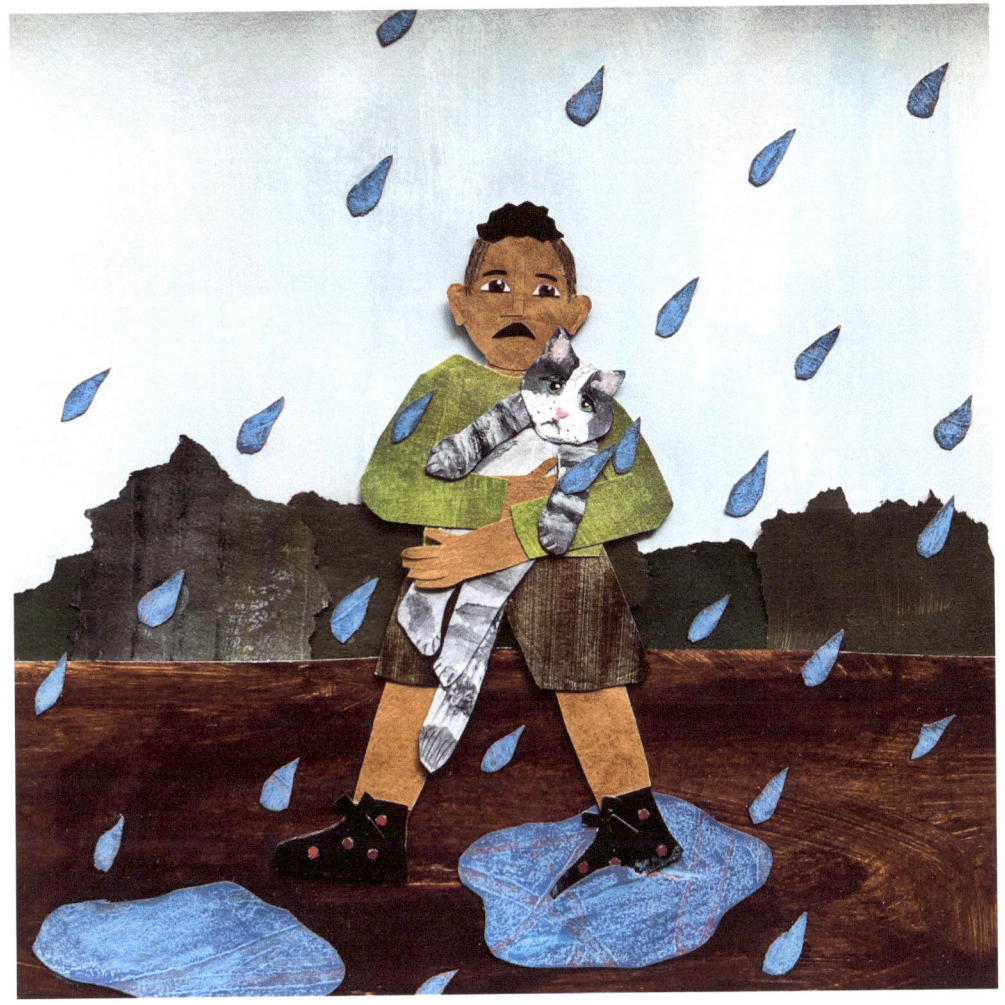

WHEN YOU TURN YOUR MOUTH DOWN.

G IS FOR GIVE

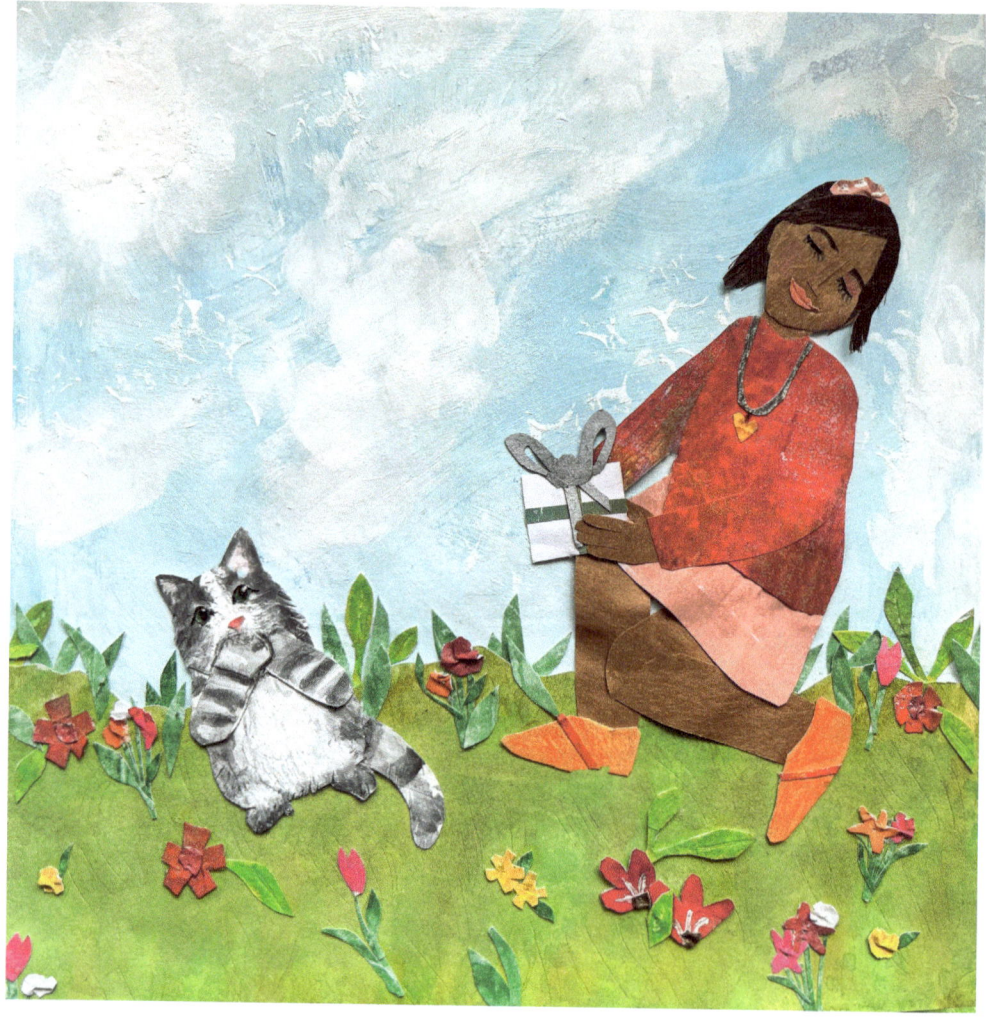

WHAT A SWEET WAY TO LIVE!

H 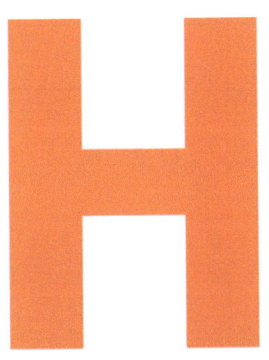 IS FOR HOP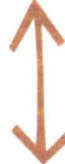

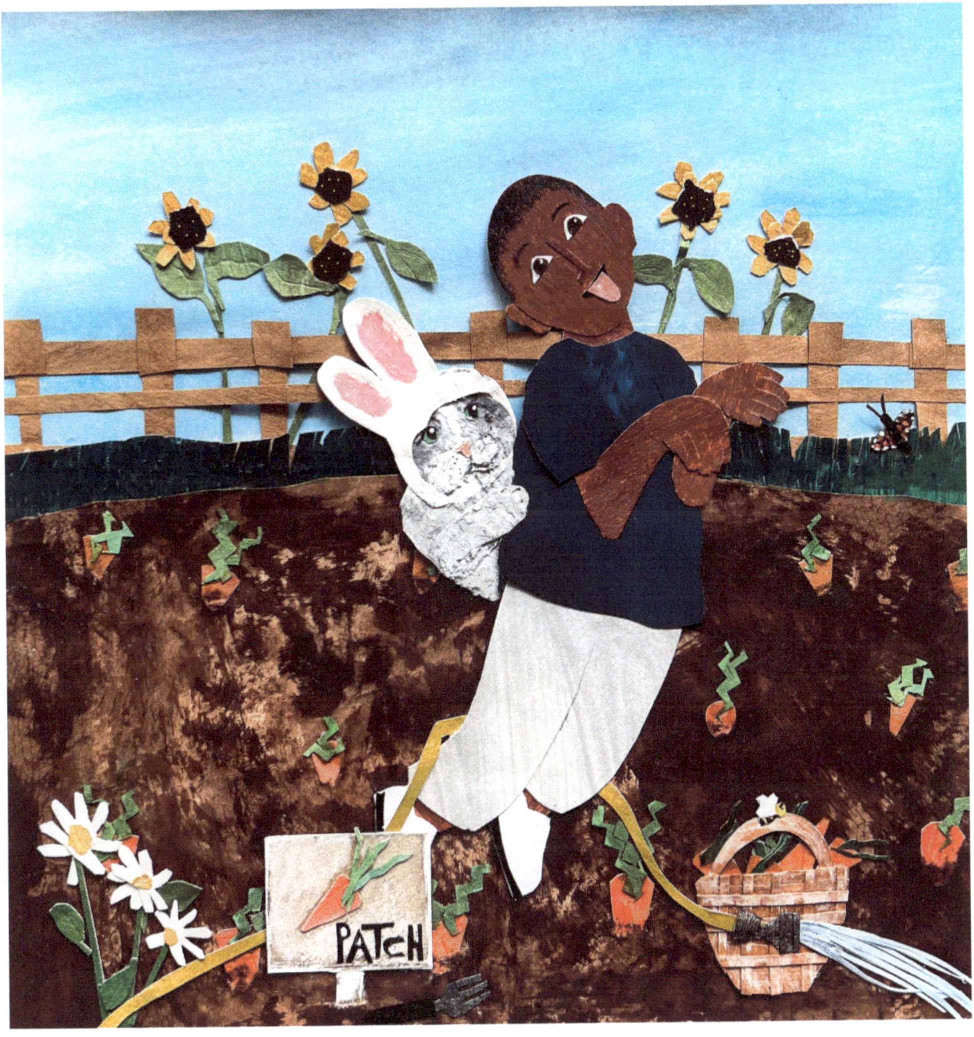

LOOK OUT FOR THE CARROT CROP!

I IS FOR IDENTIFY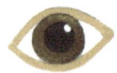

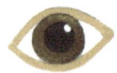

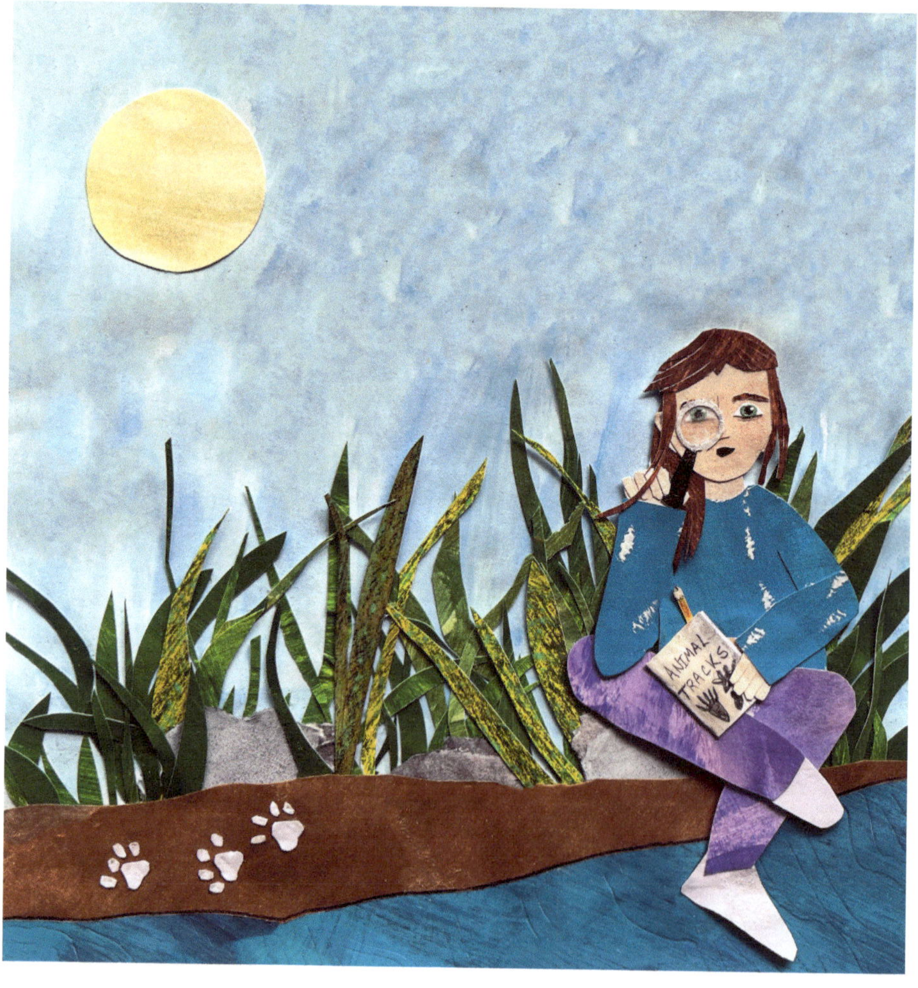

I HAVE FOOTPRINTS TO CLASSIFY.

J 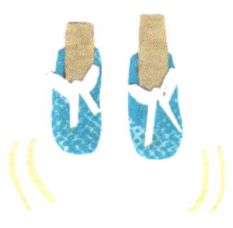 IS FOR JUMP

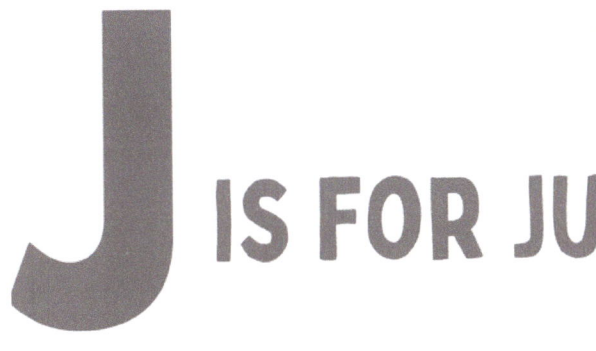

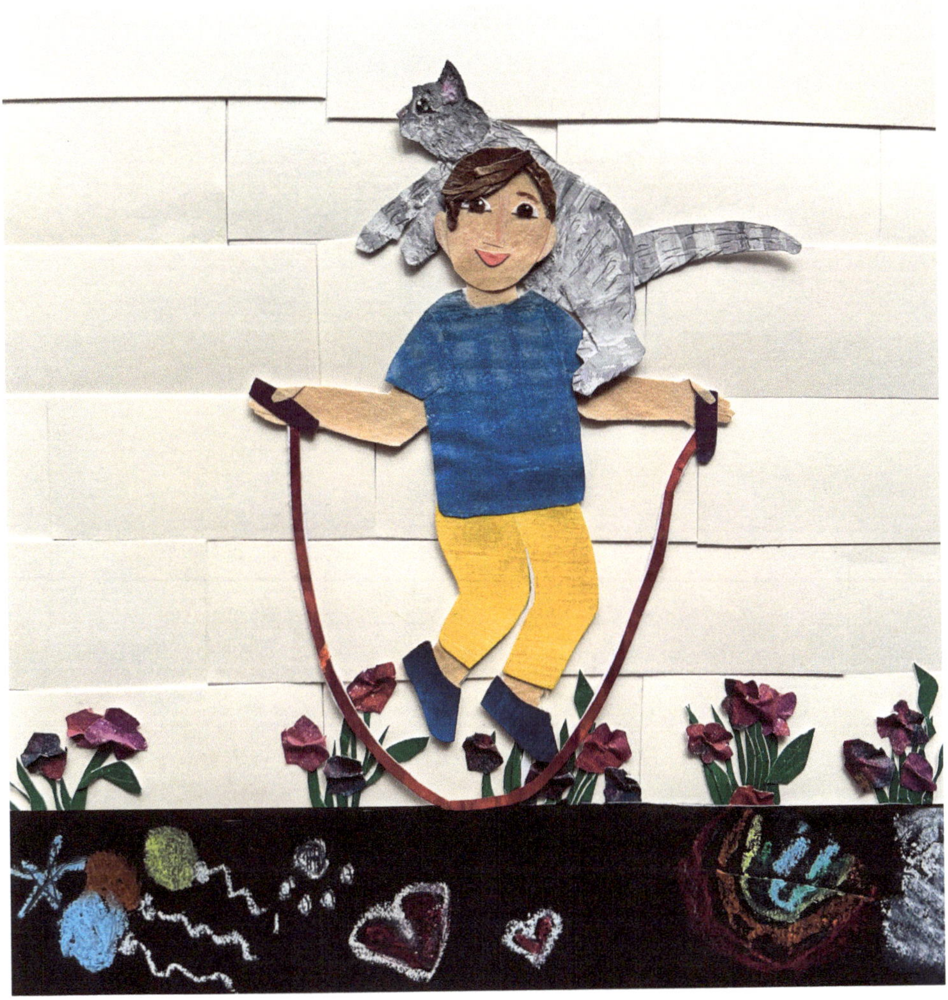

AND YOU LAND WITH A THUMP!

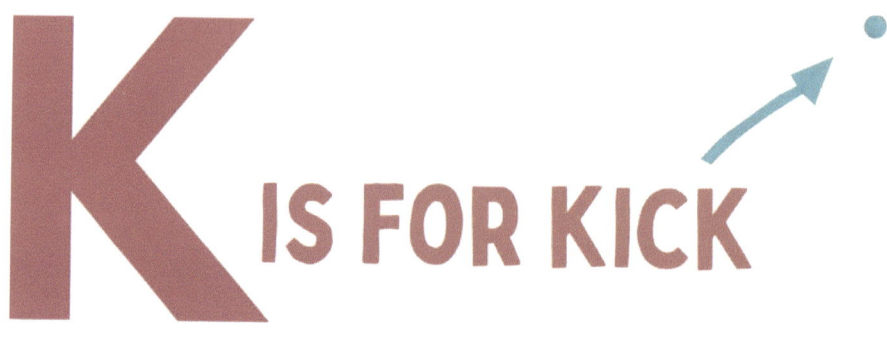

K IS FOR KICK

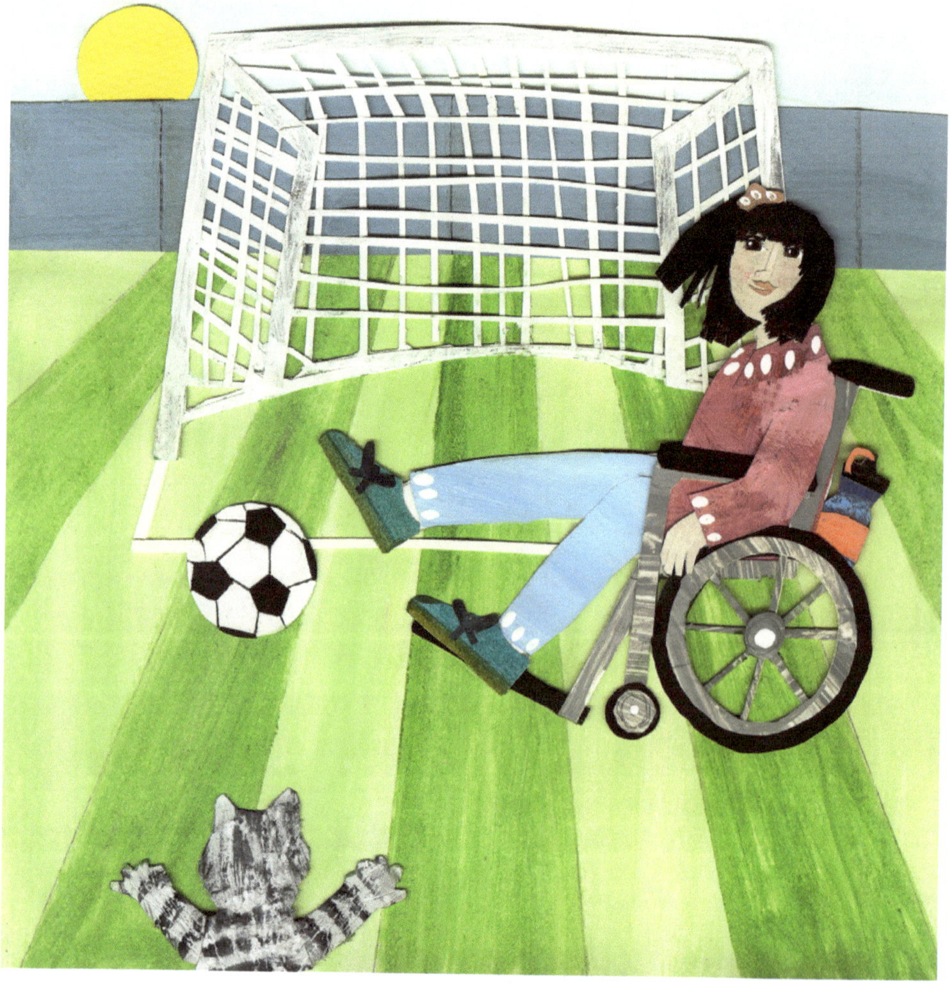

TO CATCH THE BALL YOU MUST BE QUICK.

L IS FOR LISTEN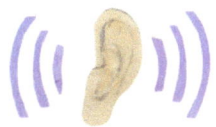

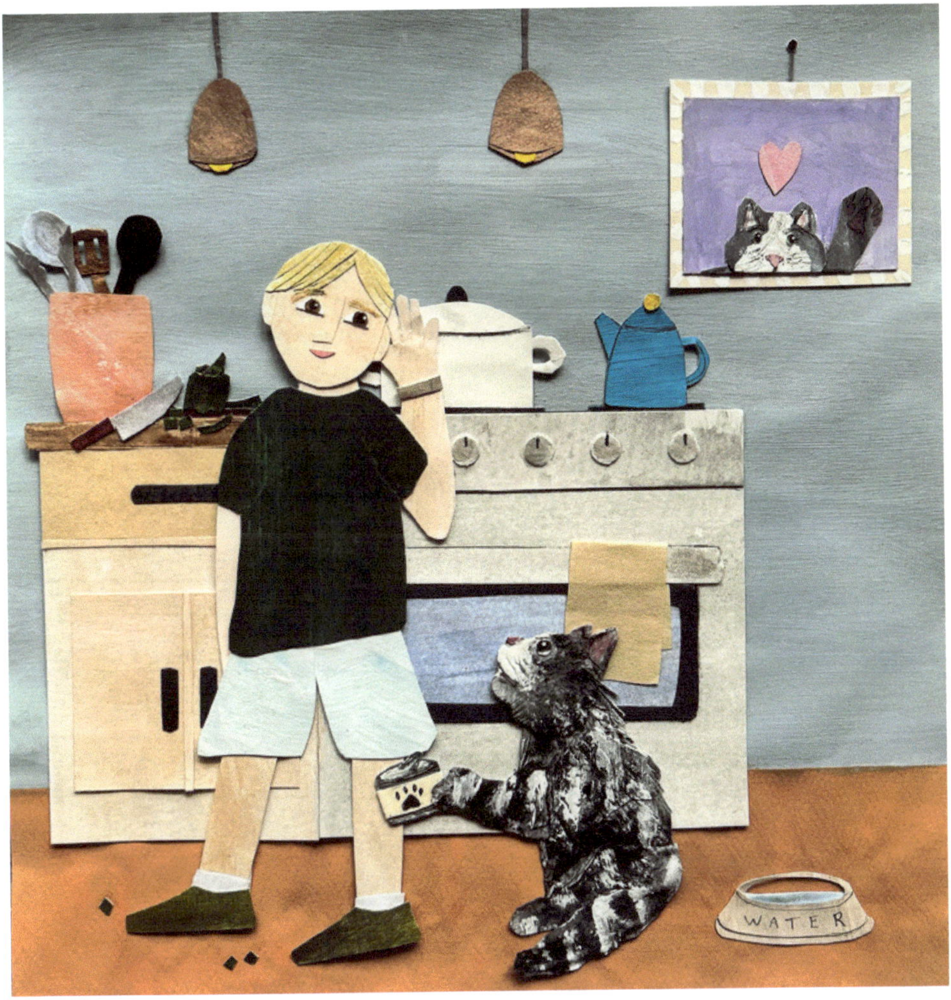

LOOK HOW MY EMPTY BOWL GLISTENS!

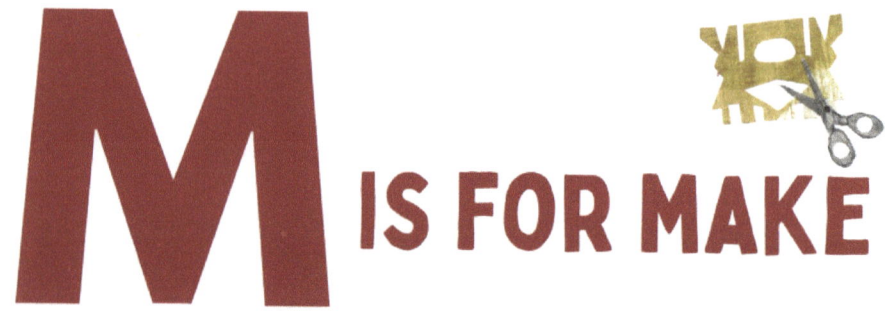

M IS FOR MAKE

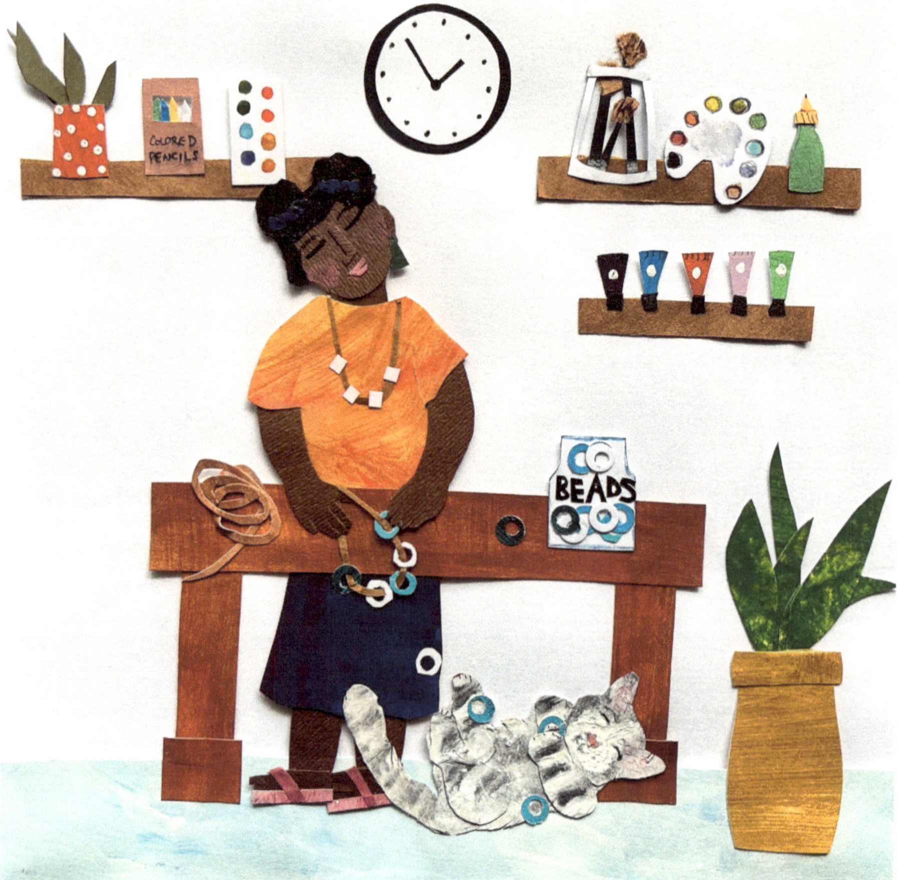

JUST HAVE FUN, THERE ARE NO MISTAKES!

N

IS FOR NAP

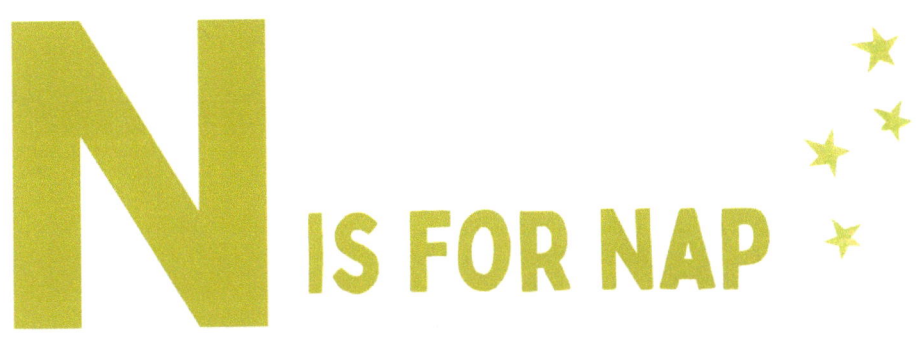

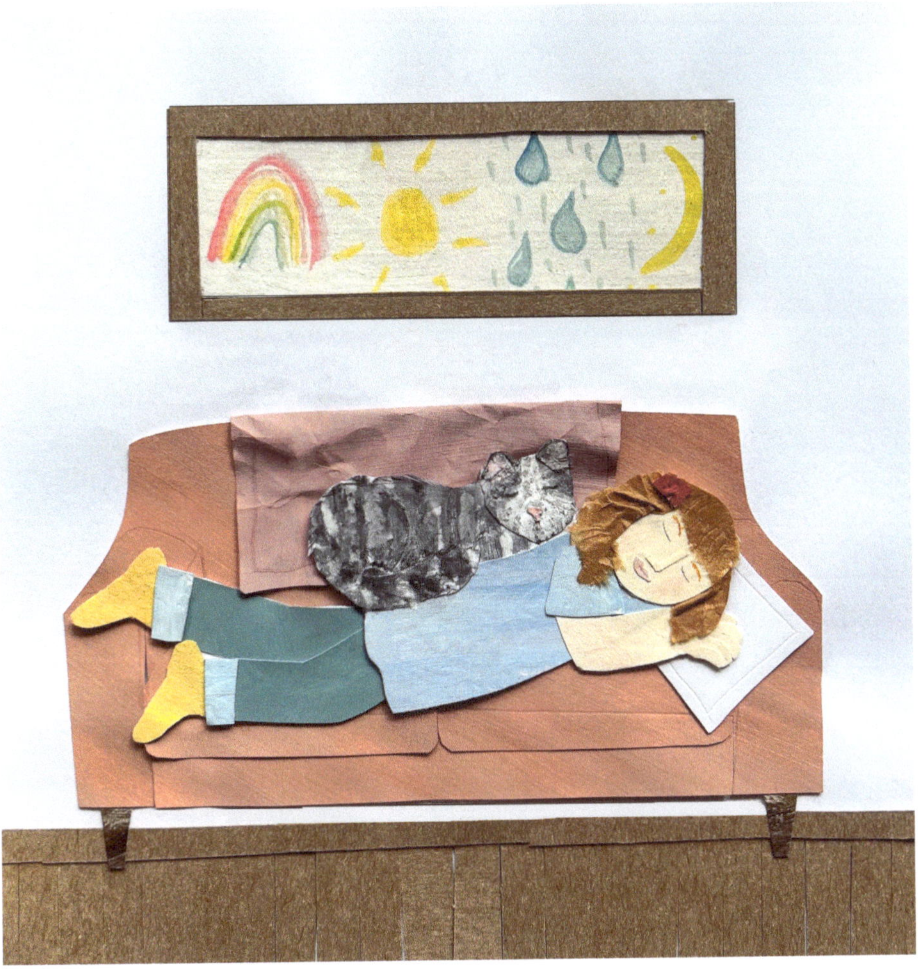

I CAN SLEEP ON A BACK OR A LAP.

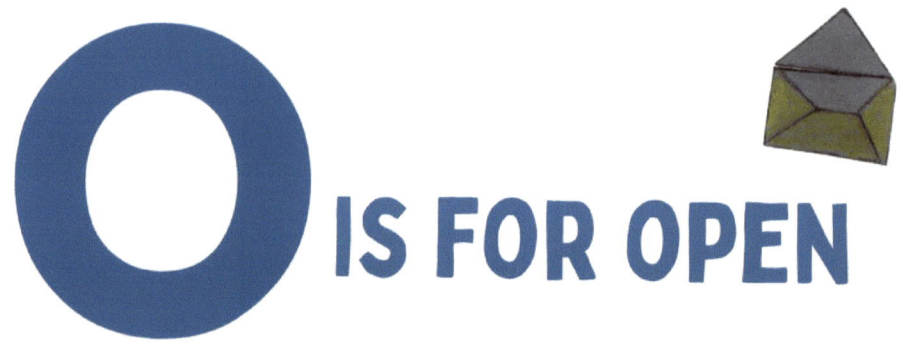

O IS FOR OPEN

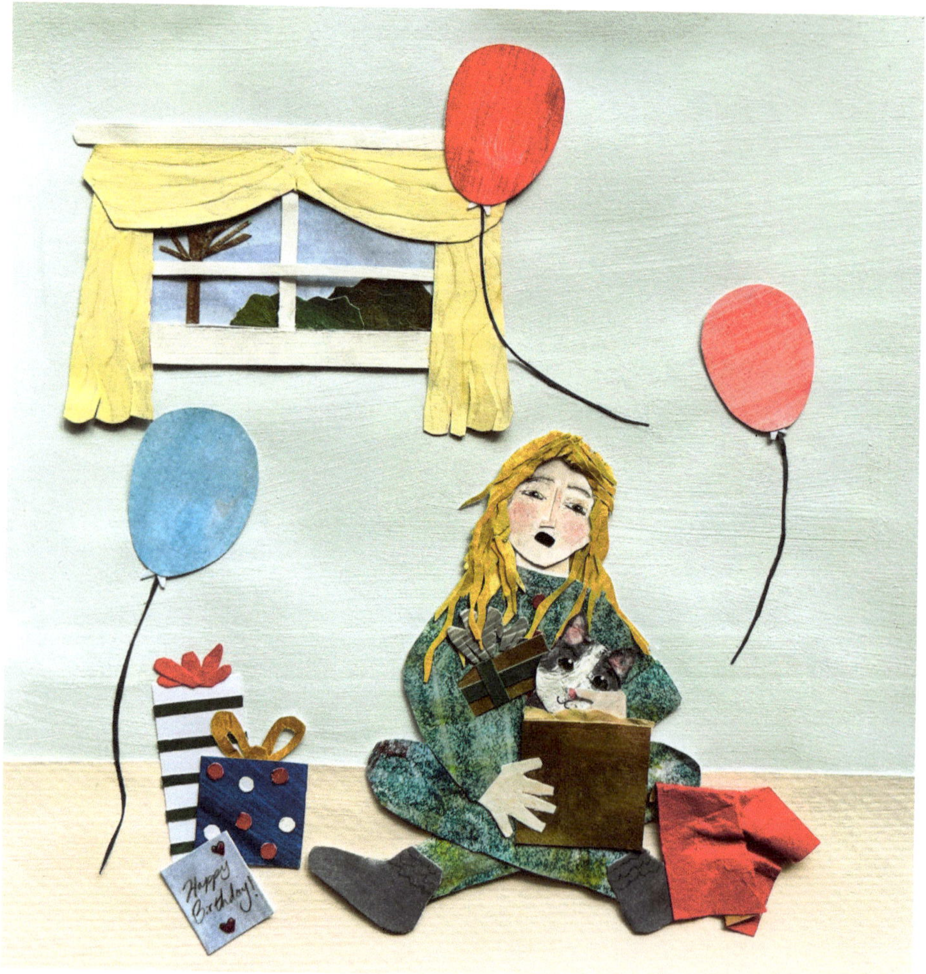

ALL THAT WISHIN' AND HOPIN'!

P IS FOR PULL

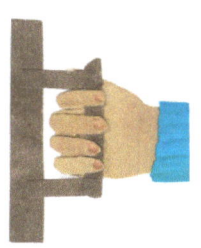

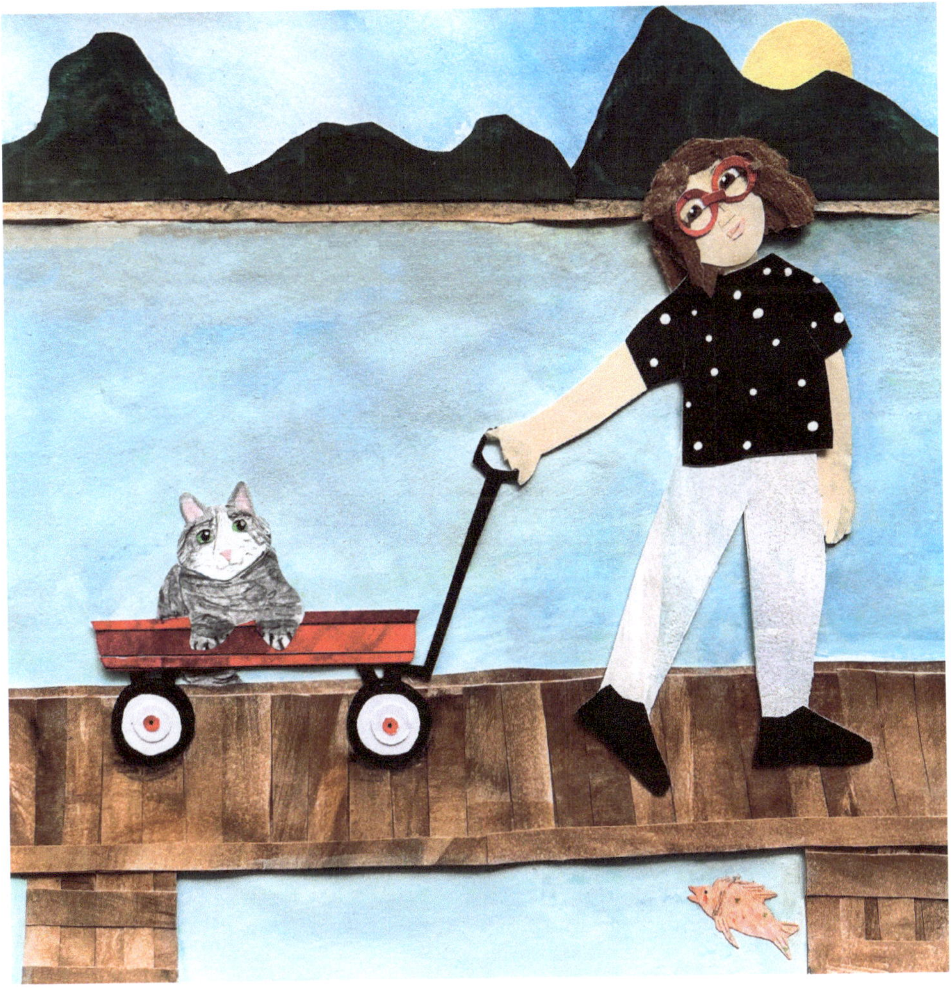

HOW DID MY WAGON GET SO FULL?

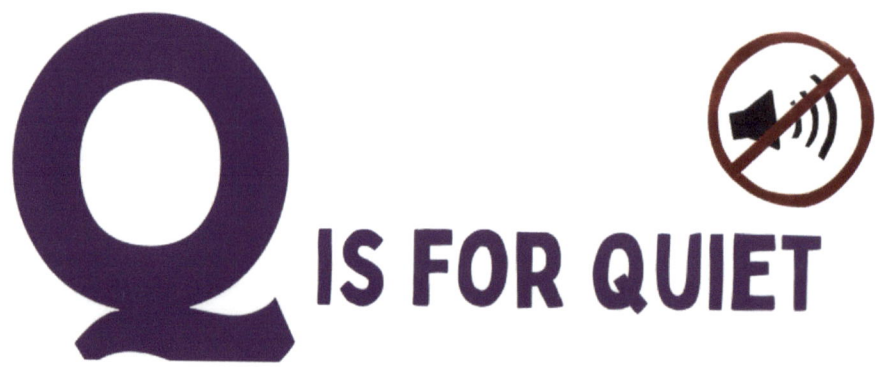

Q IS FOR QUIET

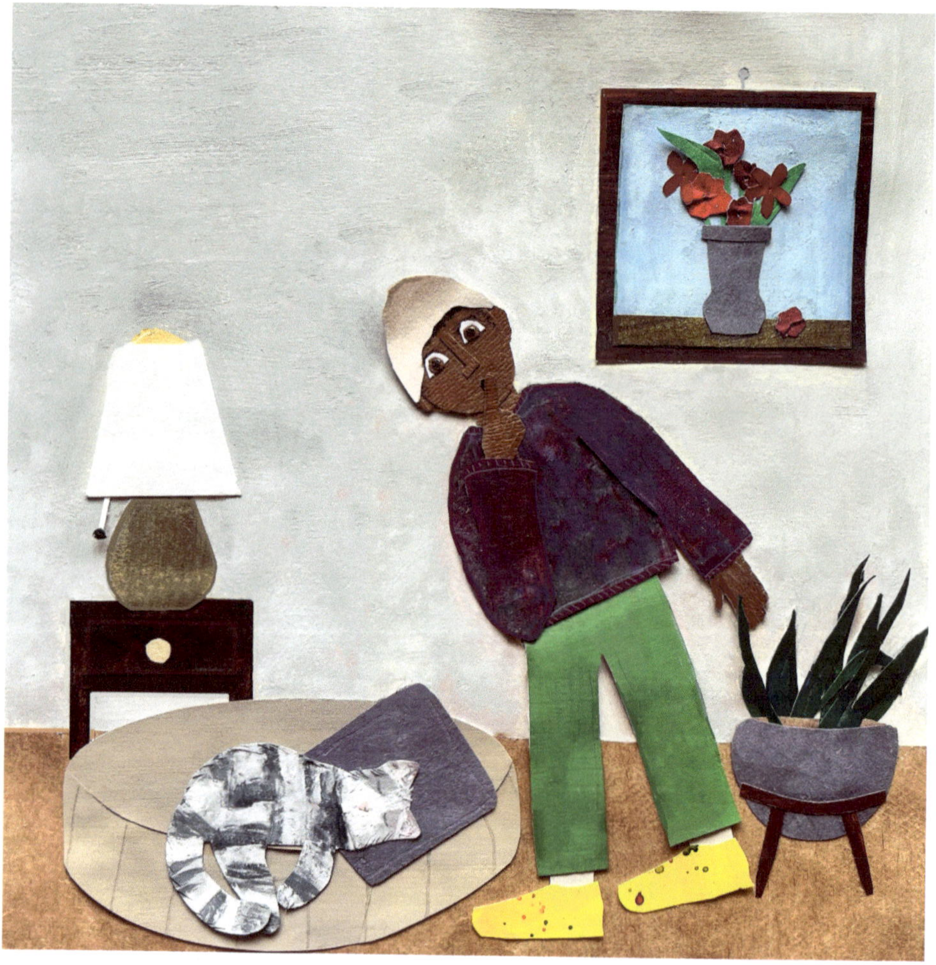

YOU COULD WAKE HIM, BUT I WOULDN'T TRY IT!

R IS FOR READ

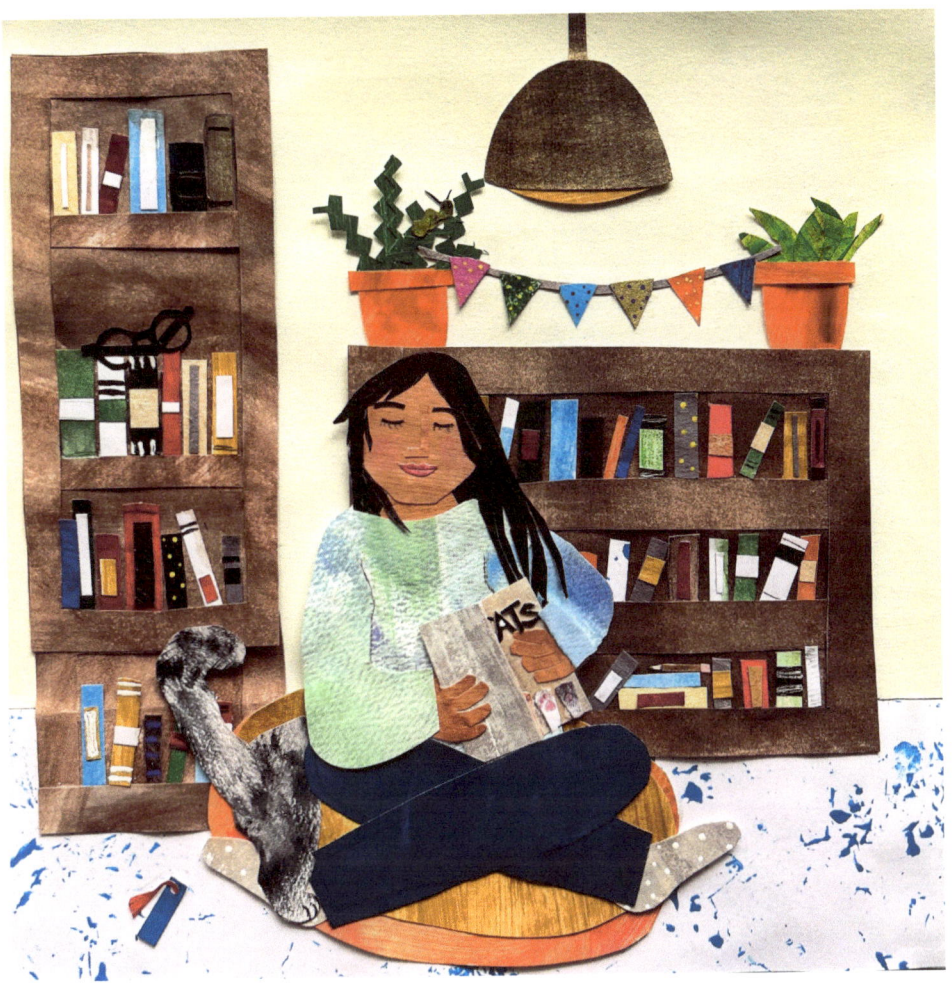

AND YOUR MIND YOU WILL FEED.

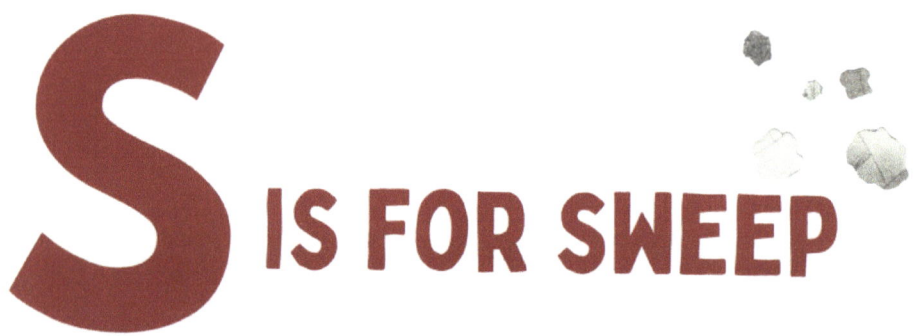

S IS FOR SWEEP

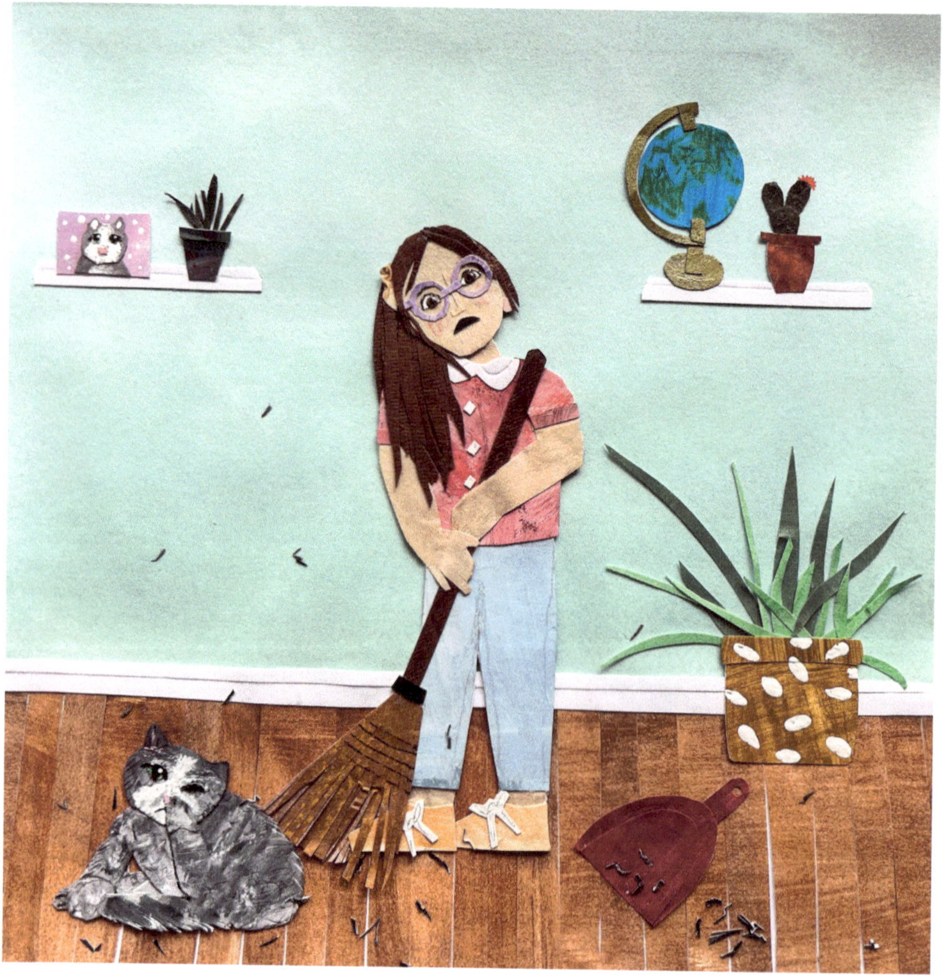

CLEAN FOR NOW, BUT IT WILL NEVER KEEP!

T IS FOR THROW

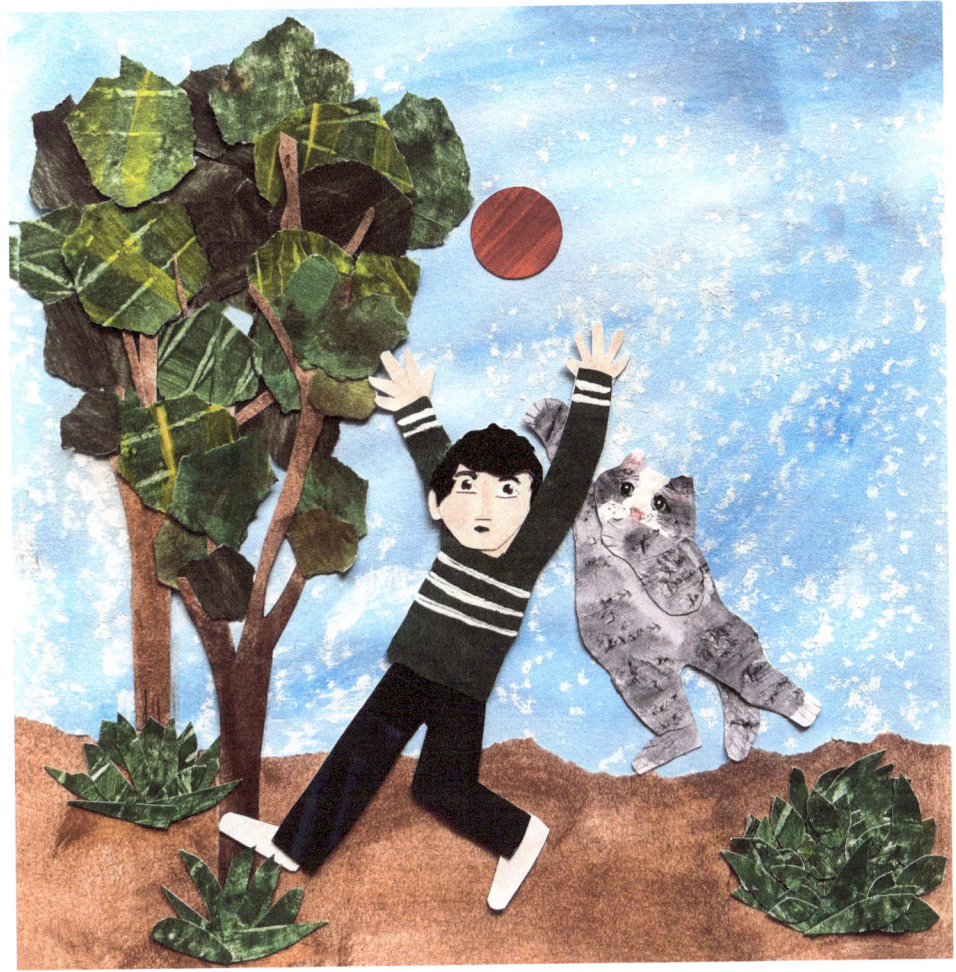

MAKE IT GO HIGH NOT LOW!

U

IS FOR UNLOCK

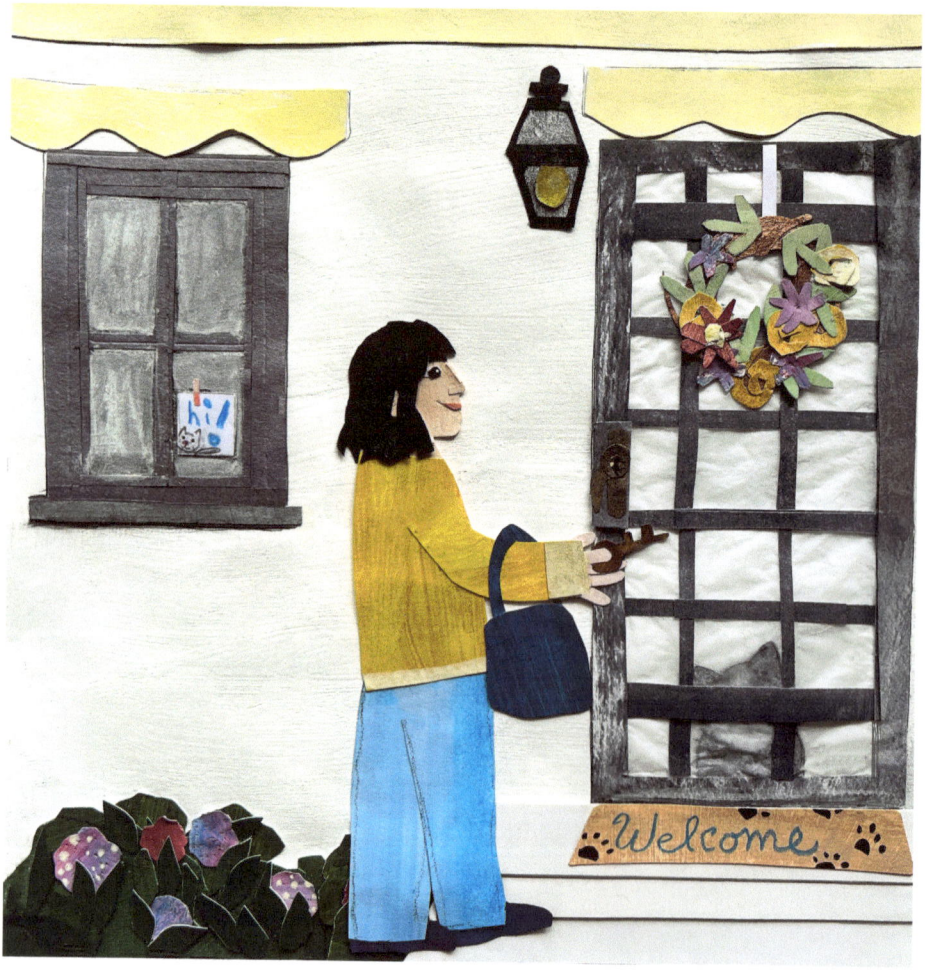

I HAVE A KEY, NO NEED TO KNOCK!

V IS FOR VOTE

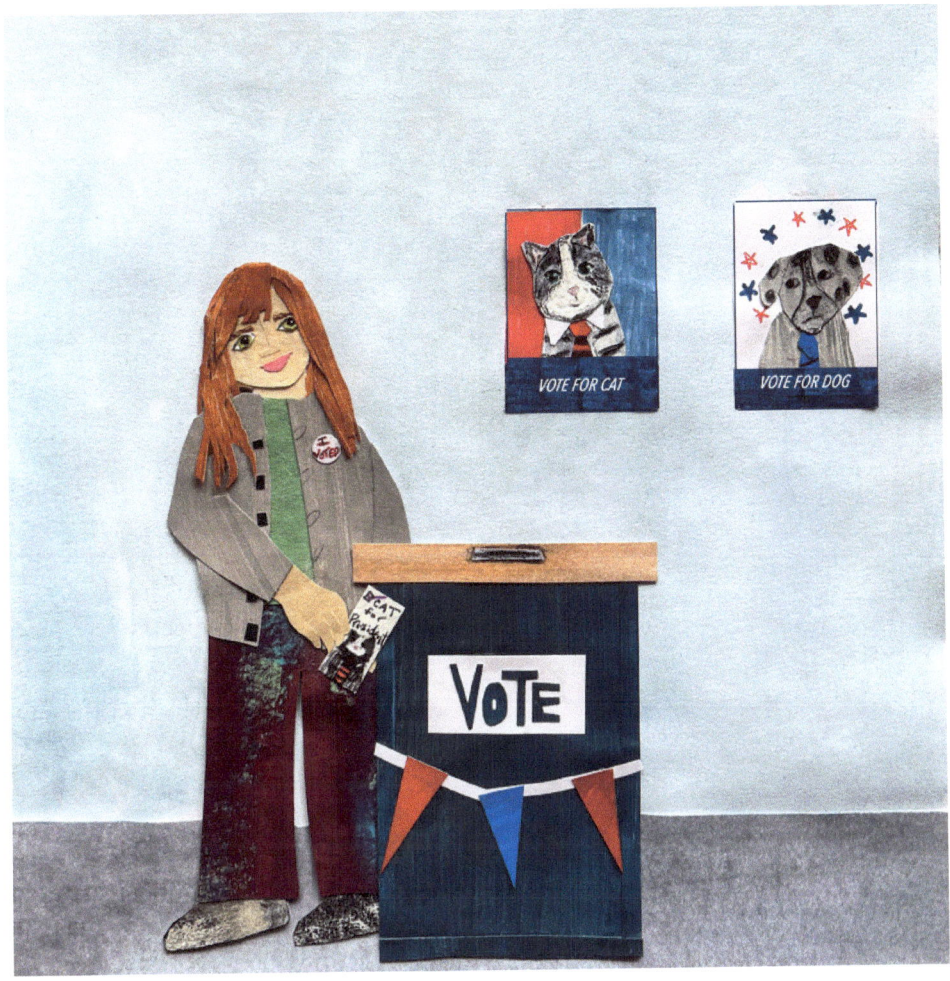

SO HER FAVORITE SHE WROTE.

W IS FOR WHISPER

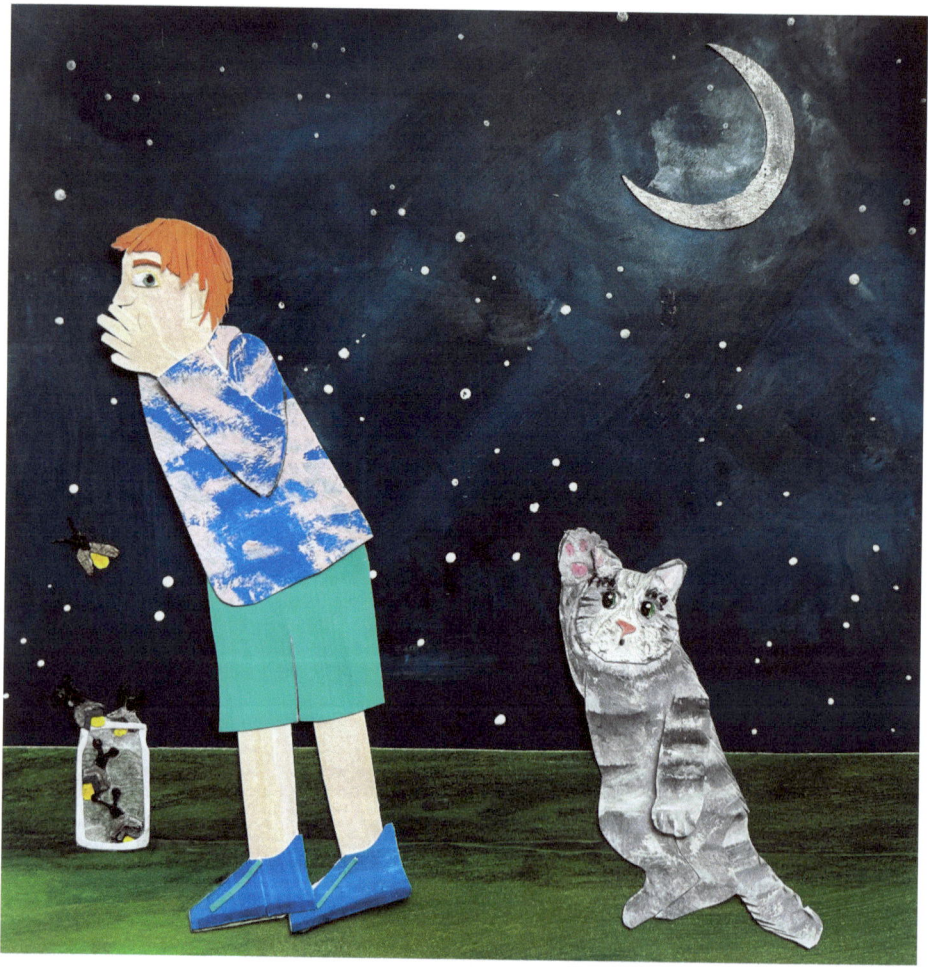

HEY! CAN YOU SPEAK UP, MISTER?

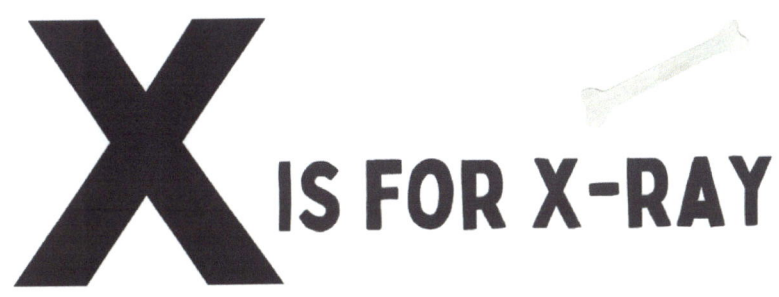

X IS FOR X-RAY

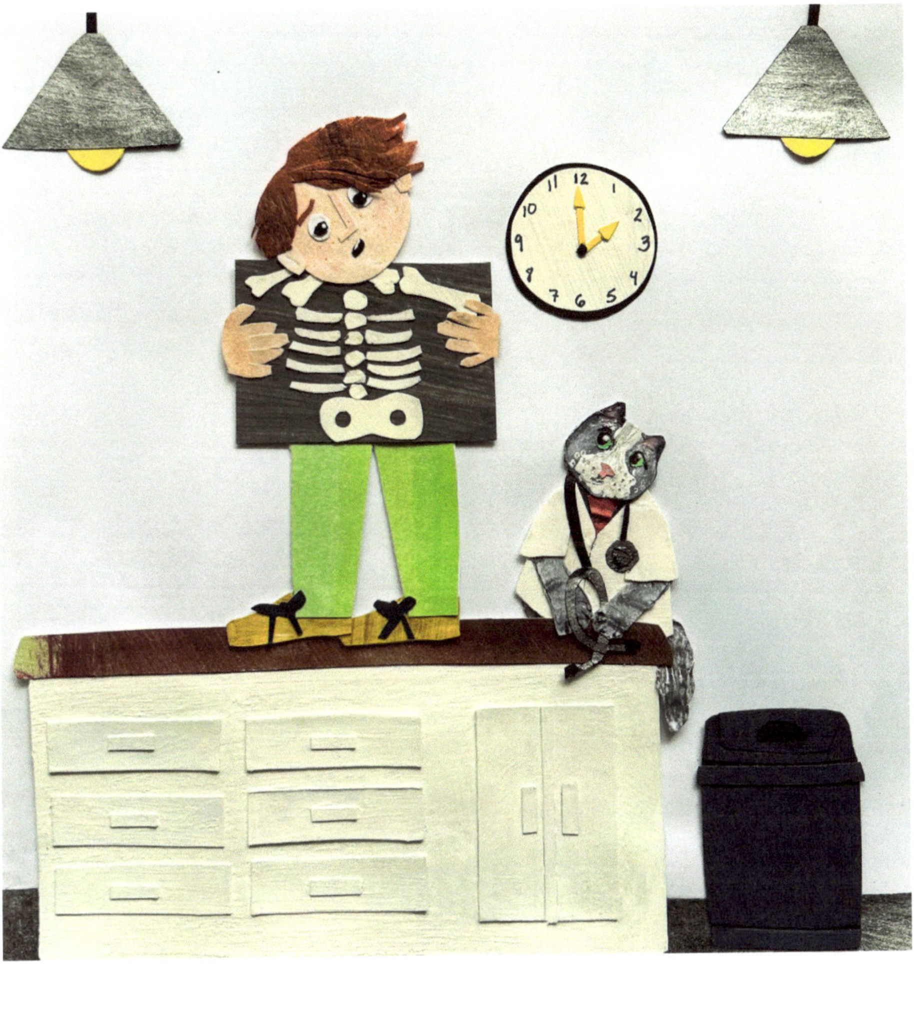

OH, WHAT A DISPLAY.

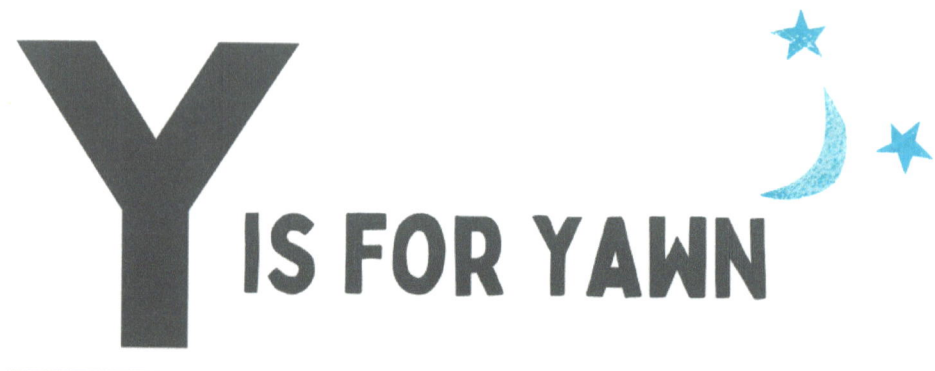

Y IS FOR YAWN

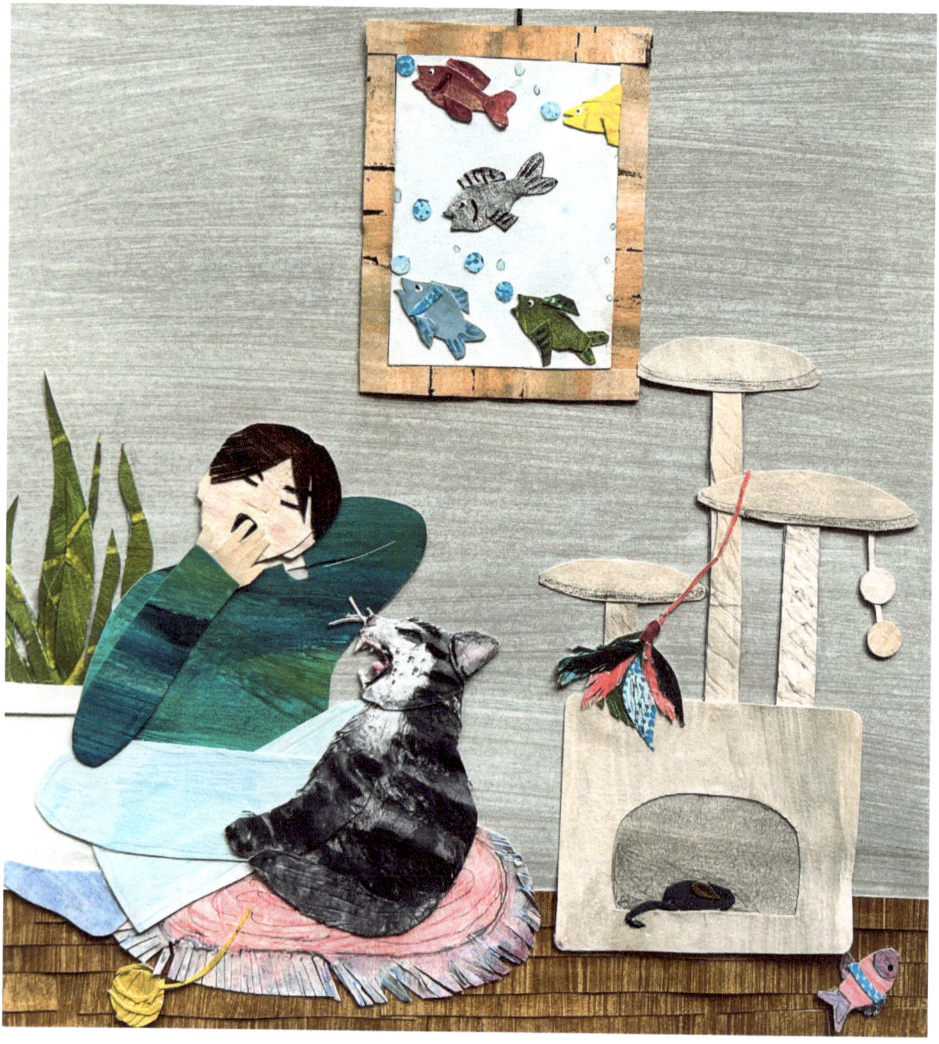

I COULD SLEEP UNTIL DAWN.

Z IS FOR ZOOM

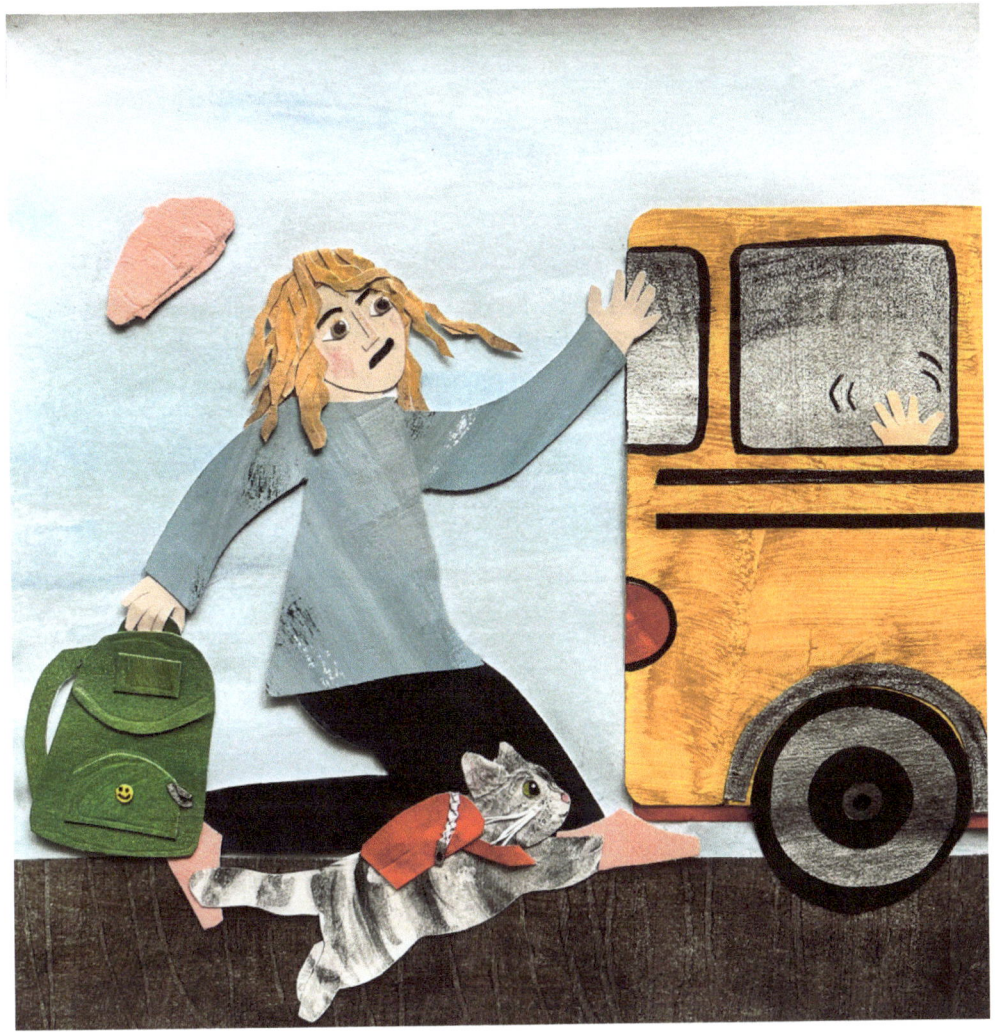

THE BOOK IS DONE, IT'S TIME TO GO VROOM!

THE END.

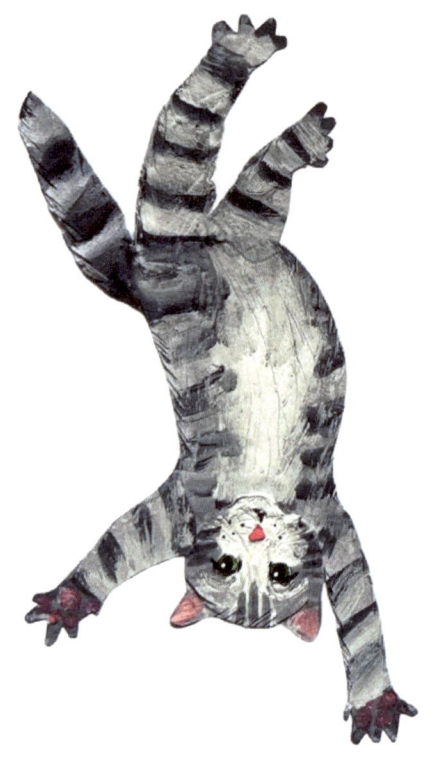

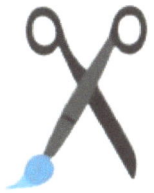

LAURA HOMSEY is a paper artist
with a background in K-12 arts education.

She has illustrated hundreds of portraits
for families and businesses in her
favorite medium, hand-cut paper.

This is her first book.

Visit her online at
www.petitpaperstories.com